The Little Book of Contentment

The Little Book of Contentment

*A Guide to Becoming Happy with Life and Who
You Are, While Getting Things Done*

Leo Babauta

WAKING LION PRESS

ISBN 978-1-4341-0399-4

Published by Waking Lion Press, an imprint of The Editorium. Waking Lion Press™, the Waking Lion Press logo, and The Editorium™ are trademarks of The Editorium, LLC.

The Editorium, LLC
West Jordan City, UT 84081-6132
wakinglionpress.com
wakinglionpress@editorium.com

This book is written for my wife Eva, who is beautiful but doesn't know it, and my daughter Chloe, who deserves to be happy but doesn't feel it in her heart yet.

Contents

THE AGREEMENT   ix

THE ROOT OF THE PROBLEM   1

THE WHAT AND WHY OF CONTENTMENT   5

THE PATH OF CONTENTMENT   7

CONTENTMENT ISN'T DOING NOTHING   11

COMPARING TO WHAT YOU DON'T HAVE   15

WATCH YOUR IDEALS AND EXPECTATIONS   17

ADVERTISING AND FANTASIES   21

BUILD TRUST   25

LOVE YOURSELF   31

TRYING TO FIND HAPPINESS IN EXTERNAL SOURCES   35

WHERE HAPPINESS COMES FROM	41
FINDING HAPPINESS WITHIN	45
OUR REACTIONS TO THE ACTIONS OF OTHERS	49
DON'T TIE YOUR SELF-WORTH TO OTHERS' ACTIONS	55
BECOME WHOLE IN A RELATIONSHIP	61
SELF-HAPPINESS AND MEETING OTHERS	67
JEALOUSY OF OTHERS	71
TECHNIQUES FOR SELF-ACCEPTANCE	73
FREQUENTLY ASKED QUESTIONS	79
CONCLUSION	95
SUMMARY OF ACTION STEPS	99
FOR MORE	105

The Agreement

This isn't meant to be a book that you glance through and then set aside. It's also not about general philosophy or life advice. It's not meant to get you to buy into a program.

What is this book for then?

It's meant for action. The intent of this book is for you to:

1. Read it in an hour. Not put aside, but actually read it.

2. Put the method into action. Immediately.

3. Practice the skills daily, just a few minutes a day. In a short time, you should have some basic skills that help you to be content, less angry, less stressed out.

How does that sound? If you're happy with that, let's make an agreement:

1. You do those three things.

2. You also agree to close everything else on your computer and give yourself an hour of undistracted time to read this book.

3. I agree to keep things short, to make the most of your time, and to teach you some really useful skills.

With that out of the way, I am incredibly glad you're here. Thanks for reading.

The Root of the Problem

Almost every kind of problem we have has discontent with ourselves (and our lives) as its root.

I'll repeat that for emphasis: *All of our problems stem from discontent.*

Let's take a look at a variety of examples:

1. *Addicted to food*: Food gives you temporary happiness, you seek happiness from external sources because you aren't happy with yourself. The pleasure from food is temporary, making you a bit depressed that you ate so much junk, making you unhappier, causing you to seek comfort from the food.

2. *Addicted to cigarettes, drugs, pills, alcohol*: Same reason as food addiction, same cycle.

3. *Addicted to the Internet, video games, porn*: See above.

4. *Debt and clutter*: You buy things as a source of external happiness (see above), and are afraid of what will happen if you let go of those things. This is a lack of confidence that you'll be OK with nothing but yourself.

5. *Afraid to meet people*: You are afraid of how other people might judge you because you are not confident about who you are, because you are unhappy with who you are.

6. *Afraid to start your own business*: You are afraid you'll fail because you don't have confidence in yourself, because you are unhappy with who you are.

7. *Unhappy with your body*: You want your body to meet some ideal, and of course it doesn't. You can't accept that your body is perfect just as it is (though of course improving your health is always good), and that people will love you for who you are, no matter how your body looks.

8. *Fail at creating new habits*: You don't really believe you can stick to the habits because you have failed so often before so you don't give it your full effort. You don't trust yourself, and so you think you're not a reliable, disciplined, good person.

9. *Jealous, insecure about boyfriend/girlfriend, check their Facebook page to see who they're flirting with*: You don't

really believe your significant other will want to stay with you, and believe they'll abandon you, because you don't think you're good enough.

10. *Jealous about what other people are doing on Facebook/Instagram, worried that you're missing out*: You think everyone else is having more fun than you, because you are unhappy with what you're doing right now—it's not good enough; but at the heart it's because you think you're not awesome enough.

11. *Procrastinate/distracted by Internet*: You get the urge to do something easier, more comfortable, rather than stick with something tough, uncomfortable; you don't want to do the uncomfortable because it's hard and you think you'll fail; you don't trust yourself to stick to something that's hard.

12. *Anxiety*: You have an ideal outcome that you really want to happen, and the anxiety comes from the fear that the outcome won't happen. Holding onto this ideal outcome happens because you don't think you'll be OK if other unexpected outcomes happen; because you don't have confidence in yourself.

13. *Anger*: You have an ideal outcome you really want to happen, and you are angry when someone else prevents that from happening. Holding onto this ideal outcome happens because you don't think you'll be

OK if other unexpected outcomes happen, because you don't have confidence in yourself.

I could go on, with another 20 examples, but you can see how many of these problems are really the same problem in different forms, and in the end there are a few key ideas that are repeated in many of the problems.

The key problems associated with discontent:

1. An ideal/fantasy we are holding onto.

2. Unhappiness with who we are.

3. Lack of trust/confidence in ourselves.

4. Seeking happiness externally.

Action step: Think about which of the above (and other) problems you might have. Can you see the root of discontent with yourself (and your life) in each problem?

The What and Why of Contentment

What is contentment? For me, it's really about being happy with who you are. Which I wasn't for many years, and I think most people are not.

In my life, I've learned to be better at the skill of contentment. I am happy with my life. I am happy with myself. I'm happy with where I am professionally, and I don't seek to add more readers or page views or income. I'm happy wherever I am.

Many might say, "Sure, you can say that now that you've reached a certain level of success," but I think that's wrong. Many people who achieve success don't find contentment, and are always driven to want more and are unhappy with themselves. Many people who are poor or don't have a "successful" career have found contentment. And what's more,

I think finding contentment has actually driven any success that I've found—it helped me get out of debt, it helped me change my habits, it has made me a better husband, father, friend and collaborator—perhaps even a better writer.

Worst of all, with the attitude of "you can be content because you're successful," is that people who say this are dismissing the path of contentment . . . when it's something they can do right now. Not later, when they reach certain goals or a certain level of financial success. Now.

Action step: Ask yourself if you're content right now. If not, when do you want to be content? What's stopping you?

The Path of Contentment

We start out in life thinking that we're awesome. We can dance in public as 5-year-olds and not care what others think of us. By the time we're adults, that's been driven out of us, by peers and parents, and the media and embarrassing situations.

As adults, we doubt ourselves. We judge ourselves badly. We are critical of our bodies, of ourselves as people, of our lack of discipline, of all our faults. We don't like our lives.

As a result, we try to improve this lacking self, try to get better because we suck so much. Or we doubt our ability to get better and are unhappy about that. Or we sabotage our attempts at change because we don't really believe we can do it.

This self-dislike results in worse relationships, a stagnant career, unhappiness with life, complaints about everything, and often unhealthy habits, such as eating junk food, drinking too much alcohol, not exercising, shopping too much, being addicted to video games or the Internet.

So what's the path to being content with yourself and your life?

The first problem is if you don't trust yourself. That's an important area to work with.

Your relationship with yourself is like your relationship with anyone else. If you have a friend who is constantly late and breaking his word, not showing up when he says he will, eventually you'll stop trusting that friend. It's like that with yourself, too. It's hard to like someone you don't trust, and it's hard to like yourself if you don't trust yourself.

So work on this trust with yourself (I give some practical steps in the bottom section below). Increase it slowly, and eventually you'll trust yourself to be awesome.

The second problem is that you judge yourself badly. You compare yourself to an unreal ideal, in all areas. You want a beautiful model's body. You want to achieve certain goals, personally and professionally. You want to travel the world and learn languages, and learn a musical instrument, and be an amazing chef, and have an amazing social life, and have the perfect spouse and kids, and incredible achievements, and be the fittest person on the planet. Of course, those are completely realistic ideals, right?

And when we have these ideals, we compare ourselves to them, and we always measure up badly.

The path to contentment, then, is to stop comparing ourselves to these ideals. Stop judging ourselves. Let go of the ideals. And gradually learn to trust ourselves.

Action step: Consider what ideals you have that you compare yourself to. Also ask yourself if you trust yourself to be able to follow through, to stick to changes, to get things done.

Contentment Isn't Doing Nothing

Before we get to the practical steps, let's talk about contentment and change. Many people think that if you're content, you're just going to lay around doing nothing all day. Why do anything if you're content with the way things are? How does contentment mesh with self-improvement?

But contentment actually is a much better place from which to start making changes (self-improvement) than an unhappiness with who you are.

Most of us are driven by the need or desire to improve ourselves, to fix certain things about ourselves that we don't like. While that can definitely be a place for driving some changes, it's not a good place to start from with those kinds of changes.

If you feel there's something wrong with you that needs to be improved, you're going to be driven to improve yourself, but you may or may not succeed. Let's say you fail in your habit change. Then you start to feel worse about yourself, and you're then on a downward spiral, where every time you try to improve, you fail, and so you feel worse about yourself, and so on. You start to sabotage your changes, because you really don't believe that you can do them. Based on past evidence, you don't trust yourself that you can do it. And that makes you feel worse.

That's if you fail. But let's say you happen to succeed, and you're really good at succeeding. So maybe you lose weight, and then maybe you don't feel as bad about your body now.

But what happens is, if you start with the mindset of fixing what's wrong with you, it doesn't end once you have a successful change. You keep looking for what else is wrong with you, what else you need to improve. Maybe now feel like you don't have enough muscles, or nice enough abs, or you think your calves don't look good, or if it's not about your body, you'll find something else.

So it's this never-ending cycle for your entire life. You never reach it. If you start from a place of wanting to improve yourself and feeling stuck, even if you're constantly successful and improving, you're always looking for happiness from external sources. You don't find the happiness from within so you look to other things.

If you're externally looking for happiness, it's easy to get too into food, or shopping, or partying, or overwork, to try to be happy.

If instead you can find contentment within and not need external sources of happiness, you'll have a reliable source of happiness. I find that to be a much better place to be.

A lot of people wonder, "If you find contentment, won't you just lay on the beach, not improving the world, not doing anything?" But I think that's a misunderstanding of what contentment is.

You can be content and lay around, but you can also be content and want to help others. You can be content and also compassionate to others, and want to help them. You can be happy with who you are, but at the same time want to help other people and ease their suffering. And that way, you can offer yourself to the world and do great works in the world, but not necessarily need that to be happy.

Even if for some reason, your work was taken away from you, you'd still have that inner contentment.

Action step: Think about the things about yourself that you want to change. Then see if, instead, you can find things about yourself you're really happy with.

Comparing to
What You Don't Have

One of the biggest sources of discontent is comparing yourself to other people, or your life to what you see others doing. Or what you've accomplished compared to what others have done.

I find people comparing themselves to me all the time: they want to be as successful, or as simple, or as happy with their families, or as bald. (OK, the last one isn't true.)

Of course, they are comparing themselves to a fantasy. In real life, I'm not what they think I am. And in reality, no one you see is what you think they are—you only see certain parts of the story, the good parts, and rarely see the person's doubt and anguish and discontent. People don't share their warts and hemorrhoids, just the great pictures of their food and vacation and children.

So you're comparing yourself to a fantasy, an illusion, and of course the reality of your life (and who you are) comes up wanting. This exercise is worse than useless—it's actually harming you because you are less content as a result of the comparison.

Whenever you find yourself comparing the good parts of someone else's life to the bad parts of yours, or thinking what you could be doing instead, stop yourself. Just stop. You are actively hurting yourself, and that's not a compassionate act.

Instead, look at what you're doing right now, and be happy with that. What you're doing now can be (and probably is) amazing. Appreciate the gift of this moment. It's a miracle.

Action step: Think about the times you've compared yourself to others, and what others are doing, especially recently. Where did you get the image of others that you're comparing yourself to? Social media or apps, news, blogs, movies, magazines?

Watch Your Ideals
and Expectations

Our lives are a series of fantasies—ideals and expectations—but unfortunately we're not often aware that we're having them.

And while we all have fantasies, and sometimes they can be nice, the problem comes when life doesn't live up to the fantasy.

Reality is amazing, but when we compare it to the fantasy (which isn't real, of course), it doesn't measure up. As amazing as reality is, in all its glory, it falls short if we expect it to be some fantasy. This is a big reason we're unhappy with ourselves. It's a reason we're unhappy with others, with our lives.

It's also the reason we seek happiness in external things—we have fantasies about how great they're going to be, how incredible our lives will be once we have these external things, how happy we'll be once we have them. It's not true, though, and when we get those external things (food, a boyfriend, new clothes, etc.), they fall short and don't make us as happy as we'd hoped. And we don't learn: We keep fantasizing, keep repeating the cycle.

Some examples of our fantasies:

- We see someone with a nice body and fantasize about getting abs like that, or arms like that.

- We want a boyfriend/spouse who will make us happy, love us unconditionally, be romantic, care for our every need.

- We fantasize about forming new habits and never messing up, and having discipline.

- We fantasize that other people will be polite to us, never cut us off in traffic, never get angry, wash their dishes, and clean up after themselves.

- We fantasize about having the perfect peaceful, productive morning.

- We fantasize that other people will always care about our stories, want to hear everything we have to say, care about our needs before all else.

Of course, we don't always know we're having those fantasies. But when we get frustrated, disappointed, irritated, or angry with other people or ourselves, that's a sure sign we had a fantasy that didn't come true.

- We are discontented with ourselves because we don't meet the fantasies we have about ourselves: that we should have perfect bodies, the perfect spouse, the perfect job, be good at everything, never mess up, have perfect habits, never procrastinate, or have the charisma of a movie star.

- We are discontented with others because they don't meet the fantasies we have about how others should behave: they should be unfailingly kind to us, happy not angry, care about us and meet our needs, never be rude or cold or ignore us, and always clean up after themselves and be on time.

- We are discontented with our lives because our fantasies about how life should be don't come true: that the weather be perfect, that we have a beautiful house and a great job, and always be at the center of peace and happiness and excitement, and surrounded by people who love us, and that we never lose anyone important, and that all the great things in our lives never change.

Contentment is about letting go of these fantasies, and realizing that life is amazing without them. People around us are amazing without the fantasies. We are amazing, without the fantasies.

How do we let go of the fantasies? First by shining the light of awareness on them. Watch ourselves fantasize, realize that it's happening, realize that we don't need the fantasies. Be OK with letting them go. Watch reality closely, and recognize life's awesomeness, as it is, without the fantasies.

It's there. We just need to learn to see it.

Action step: Make a note to watch when you're frustrated, disappointed, angry, stressed, unhappy . . . and to write down, at that moment, what fantasy you're having. Practice letting them go.

Advertising and Fantasies

One of the biggest reasons people buy so much, and are so discontented with their lives, is advertising. Advertising creates false needs—all of a sudden we need an iPhone or a new car or a diamond ring, just because an advertiser put the need in our heads.

Advertising is highly effective—we might not realize it, but it works on our subconscious so that we want to buy things. It plants desires in our minds, and creates a mindset that, whatever our problem, buying something is the solution. It creates the mindset that buying is the norm, and there's no other choice.

And it's everywhere. Every nook of our lives is filled with advertising these days. It's so pervasive that we have come to accept it as a fact of life, and it cannot help but have an effect on our minds. Watch TV, advertising screams at you all day long. Read a newspaper or magazine, go to a Website, and it's in every crevice. It's on our Facebook and Twitter pages, in our email, on billboards, on buses, in sports events, in public outdoor spaces, on people's clothing, in 5K races, on blimps in the sky, in podcasts, in iTunes, before a movie starts, subtly (or not so subtly) placed products inside of movies—everywhere. On Websites, it's seen as inevitable, and a site without ads is almost unheard of (very different from the Web of 15 years ago, when ads were rare).

We can defeat the forces of advertising by not buying into the fantasies they're trying to create. Don't let them create fake needs in our heads, don't let them play upon our fears.

First, we can watch less ad-supported TV, fewer ad-supported videos online, go to Websites that aren't covered by ads (or use an ad-blocker to block them), and stop reading magazines filled with ads.

But probably more importantly, we can pay closer attention to the messages they're sending us, the fantasies they're trying to create, and the fears they are playing upon. By watching this process, we can become more conscious and less susceptible to their tactics.

We can also look at the "needs" we think we have, and realize that almost all of them are made up. Made-up needs can be eliminated. All it takes is the willingness to let go.

Action step: Examine one of your made-up needs, and ask yourself why it's such an important need. Ask what would happen if you dropped it. What good would it do? Would you have more free time and more space to concentrate and create, or less stress and fewer things to check off each day? What bad things would happen—or might happen? And how likely is it that these things would happen? And how could you counteract them?

Build Trust

When we fail at habits repeatedly, we lose trust in ourselves, don't believe in our ability to stick to something, and feel guilty and sometimes disgusted with ourselves.

This is a bad state of affairs for our future habits. It's also a cause of our discontent with ourselves.

When we start a new habit, if we don't really believe in our ability to stick to it, we're less likely to succeed. We'll doubt ourselves when things get a little harder. When we feel like quitting, part of our minds will say, "Ah, I knew this would happen. This just confirms what I thought about you, you loser." And then we quit, instead of sticking it out and beating the quitting feeling.

The reasons we lose trust are rooted in self-judgment and negative beliefs about ourselves. When we happen to fail at sticking to something—which I will tell you without a doubt is inevitable, even for the most disciplined of people—we then use that as a way to judge ourselves.

We say, "What the hell, self? Why didn't you stick to that? What's wrong with you? Gosh, I really wish you could do better. You suck at sticking to things."

For some of us, that's the voice of our parents! Or one of our parents. Or perhaps a sibling, or a classmate at school, or another relative, or just a collective voice that we've put together from people criticizing us over the years.

That voice is critical (not in a good way), and it causes us to judge ourselves and not like ourselves and not trust ourselves. However: The voice is wrong. It's just a voice talking in our heads. We don't have to believe it, even if it talks.

So we fail at one habit, and then criticize ourselves. We internalize that, not as "this is just something that happened that I need to fix," but as "this is an indicator that I am unreliable, not good enough." This becomes a big data point that shows us our self-worth.

And it happens again. And yet again. Each time it happens, we feel worse about ourselves, feel less worthy, and so we make it *more likely* that we'll fail the next time. This pattern can go on for years.

How to Regain Trust

There are some skills we need to learn:

1. *Realize that failure isn't a reason to judge yourself.* This is really important, and if you learn nothing else, this is the takeaway. Instead of internalizing failure as an indicator that we are not trustworthy or not sufficient, we need to learn that failure is just an external event. Sure, we were involved with that event, but it's like throwing a ball toward a hoop—if we miss, does that mean we are horrible people? No, it just means we need to adjust the way we throw the ball. Perhaps move closer. Maybe throw underhand if that's more successful. Get a ladder. Make the hoop bigger. Find someone to help. There are no rules in this game—we can figure out ways to make ourselves succeed. *Failure is simply an indicator that something in our method needs to be changed.*

2. *Forgive yourself for past mistakes.* Before you can start to trust yourself again, you have to go over all your past failures and the bad feelings you have of them. Just take a few minutes right now to do that. Yes, you failed. Yes, that's OK. We all fail. That's no reason to feel bad about yourself. Let it go! Tell yourself that you are good, that mistakes were not your fault but rather the fault of the method.

3. *Start to make and keep promises with yourself.* This part takes longer because trust isn't regained

overnight. Make small promises to yourself. Seriously, as small as you can. For example, if your habit is yoga, tell yourself all you need to do is get on the mat. You don't even need to do 5 minutes. Then do everything you can to keep that promise. Same thing for non-habit stuff—just start writing, just get one veggie in your meal, just close your computer for a minute when a timer goes off (if you want to focus on other things besides the Internet, for example). Small promises but big efforts to keep them. Over time, you'll start to learn that you are trustworthy.

4. *Learn to get through the tough times.* There will always be times when you don't feel like doing the habit, when you feel like giving up, when you miss a day or two for various reasons, and don't feel like starting. First, recognize that these are dips in your motivation and that it will take a little extra effort to get through them. Second, recognize the negative thoughts you might be having about your ability to get through them or the rationalizations that you have to not do it, and don't listen. Third, tell yourself that all you need to do is find some extra motivation—ask a friend for help, go on a forum to ask for some accountability and encouragement, give yourself a big reward, announce a challenge just to get through this sticking point.

Four steps, none super easy but none so hard that you can't

nail them. You got this. You can trust yourself to form new habits and stick to them, and when you have that trust, nothing can stop you.

Love Yourself

One of the biggest manifestations of our fear that we're not good enough is our belief that our bodies aren't good enough.

Very few people are happy with their body.

I'll say that again for emphasis: pretty much no one is happy with their body. Not you, not me, not our beautiful relative or co-worker, not that hot girl (or guy) you saw on the street today, not even beautiful celebrities like Angelina Jolie or Brad Pitt.

We believe we are too fat, or unfit. Or we think we're too skinny, or too short, or too thick, or weird-looking. Or we're not overweight but still want to lose 10 lbs. Or maybe we need more muscle or want to be more toned. Maybe we have great bodies but not enough definition in our abs. Maybe our skin is too dark or too pasty white. Or our eyes are too close together, or our teeth are crooked or over- or under-bitten. Our hair sucks. Our toes are ugly.

Can you see what we're doing to ourselves? It's a form of self-hate, and it causes us to be depressed, insecure, discontented with ourselves—and seek external forms of happiness.

If we recognize that we are judging ourselves badly based on fantasies of how we want to be and then realize it's unhealthy and insane, we can start to reverse it.

Let's start by realizing that we have these fantasy images and unrealistic expectations. They are totally unnecessary. Let's toss them out.

Now let's look at the comparison: Why do we need to compare ourselves to others or the images we have of others (who are, after all, also flawed)? What does this do for us? It's harmful, not helpful. Let's toss this out too.

What about the judgment? Do we need to judge ourselves at all? Do we need to say, "This is good, but not this"? What if we just said, "I love all of it, without judgment"? Isn't this how we're supposed to love our children or spouses or parents—totally, unconditionally, without judgment? Can't we love our bodies the same way—totally, unconditionally, without judgment?

So then, if we toss out fantasies, expectations, comparisons and judgments, the bad feelings and bad images go with them.

When you notice these judgments, realize that they're not helping you, and that they're harming you by creating these bad images of yourself, making you insecure about yourself.

That's not to say you shouldn't try to do things that are healthy—eat healthy food, form healthy exercise habits—but you can do those things without thinking that your body sucks. You can accept your body as it is right now and still want to do healthy things out of the joy of doing them, and out of compassion for yourself.

This all takes practice, and I'm not saying you'll do it overnight. I'm still learning myself. But again, start by noticing and start letting go. Start to love your body, without judgment, without reservation, without wishing it were anything but what it is: beautiful, and you.

Action step: Take a look in the mirror. Do it naked if you can, or at least lift up your shirt and look at your torso, and then your face. What do you see? Do you notice your judgments? Do you notice what you're judging yourself on—what you're comparing yourself to? You might not realize exactly what that fantasy ideal is—but it's based on images in the media and others you've seen in your life.

Try looking at your body (and face) without judgment. Accept it for what it is, without thinking, "I wish it were different." It's not different. It's exactly how it is, and that's the perfect version of what it should be. There is no better version.

Trying to Find Happiness in External Sources

There was a time not too many years ago when I was addicted to cigarettes, junk food, TV, shopping, and more, while being unhappy and having relationship problems.

What was the common source of all these problems? I was unhappy, so I tried to find happiness in external things.

Let's take food as an example, because it's such a common symptom. I was unhappy, but I knew that food gave me pleasure—eating some cookies or French fries was pleasurable so I felt good for a few minutes. This never failed to give me a little rush of feeling good. This is a rationalization process that occurs subconsciously, without me realizing it most of the time.

Of course, after I ate them I felt guilty and unhealthy and bad about myself, and so I was even unhappier than before. And so the cycle would repeat: To feel good again, I needed to eat again.

Most of us experience this—we try to find happiness in people and things around us, instead of finding it within. And, of course, the pleasure we get from these things is not constant, only temporary, and so our happiness goes up and down depending on whether these things are giving us pleasure right now or not.

You might not realize it, but it's probably something you do in at least one area of your life. I'm going to go over some examples of external sources of happiness, though I'm not judging you or anyone else. Obviously I've done this many times and still do, and I think it's something that every human does. That doesn't mean we can't change it, though, slowly and gradually.

Here are some ways people seek happiness from people or things:

1. *Spouse or boyfriend/girlfriend.* Such a common problem. We have this ideal of what a romantic relationship should be like and expect our significant other to make us happy in various ways. We want them to be loving to us, to do romantic or sexy things, to show they care in a thousand different ways, to put our needs before anyone else's (including theirs), to always be kind and considerate and respectful. This is a fantasy, of course, and in reality when you're in

a long-term relationship with someone, the fantasy will always break down. The other person has his or her own problems to deal with, and will get angry and sad and be rude sometimes, and not always the picture perfect romantic partner. What does this mean for our happiness? Well, when they are being loving and great, we are so happy! But when they are not, we are angry or depressed or disappointed. Why don't they love us more? And so we feel we are not lovable and worry that they will reject us.

2. *Addictions.* Food, drugs, alcohol, video games, TV, something on the Internet, sex, porn. Each of these things gives us pleasure, at least temporarily, and so they are reliable ways to find a moment's happiness. We might not be able to control our partners or children or co-workers or even our jobs, but we can control these things—if we want to eat, we usually can. If we want to smoke pot or have a beer, we usually can. Of course, these things only give temporary pleasure, and so when we aren't partaking of them, we want them. We are not happy, because our happiness depends on whether we're using these things or not. And so we go back for more, and so on.

3. *Excitement and fun.* This can manifest itself in many ways: people like to go partying, dancing, drinking with friends. Or on dates with people, or out on

the prowl at a bar. Other times people seek excitement in adventure sports, or travel. There's nothing wrong with playing sports or traveling, or going out with friends, of course. But the thing to notice is whether you're looking for your happiness in these things. And when you don't have them, are you unhappy? Because you can't always have excitement every moment of your life, and when you don't, your happiness will drop.

4. *Work.* If you are a workaholic, or addicted to being busy, you might be seeking your happiness from your work. Again, there's nothing wrong with working, nor is there anything wrong with doing work you enjoy or even love. I do it, and I get satisfaction from it. But you should pay attention to what happens when you're not working—is there a feeling of withdrawal, do you crave going back to it, is it the place where you're seeking happiness? If so, then you'll only be happy when you're working.

Action steps: We will look at how to move away from external sources of happiness in the next chapter, but right now, please take a minute to consider your external sources of happiness. What gives you pleasure, makes you happy, and what happens when these things (or people) aren't available to give you that pleasure? How do you feel?

Notice yourself as you seek these forms of pleasure. Notice when you are looking to your significant other for validation or happiness. Notice what happens when you don't have them, and how your happiness might go up or down depending on what's going on externally.

Where Happiness Comes From

It's worth taking a moment to consider where happiness comes from. Is it from things like having someone love you, or eating a fantastic meal, or having a great body, or relaxing on the beach, or drinking a good cup of coffee?

No, actually. Those things all are phenomena that happen outside of us, and they don't cause the happiness. They might be correlated with happiness—they happen, and then we are happy at the same time—but it's not a cause-and-effect relationship. There's another event that's happening at the same time.

That event is what happens in our brain between the external event (a good cup of coffee) and our state of happiness.

What is this event? It's a process. Let's take a close look:

1. We drink a cup of good coffee (or read a good book, eat some delicious berries, have good sex, etc.).

2. We notice the coffee, pay attention to it. If we don't pay attention and are reading or otherwise occupied as we drink the coffee, we don't get the happiness from the coffee.

3. We appreciate the goodness in the coffee that we noticed. It's not just the noticing and paying attention—we have to accept it for what it is, and appreciate the good things about it.

4. This goodness we've noticed *causes us to be happy about life*. We are now happy about the experience of living, about life itself, because this experience is filled with goodness—even if it's just the goodness of a cup of coffee.

So that's it: *Noticing and appreciating the goodness in a cup of coffee causes us to be happy about living.* And the more we notice and appreciate about our lives (and ourselves), the happier we are.

So does this mean that happiness is really about external things, like the cup of coffee or the sex or the love from someone else? No—it's about the process that happens within. And this process can happen no matter what's going on outside. It can happen even if there are no external stimuli—because there are things inside of us that we can appreciate as well.

Let me emphasize that: All the raw material we need for happiness is inside of us. The good things we can appreciate to be happy—they are always with us, already there. And the tools for turning these raw materials into happiness are within us as well. We just need to develop them.

Action steps: Remember this truth: Noticing and appreciating the goodness in anything causes us to be happy about living. And the more we notice and appreciate about our lives (and ourselves), the happier we are.

Finding Happiness Within ✳

If external sources of happiness aren't constant or reliable, we should look internally instead. But what does that mean?

It means finding joy in how amazing you are, in your constant growth and in the learning process, in your appreciation of life and its ever-changing state, in your appreciation of solitude and connection both. These are all awesome things, and they are all within you, all the time.

What are some of the things within us that we can appreciate, that can make us happy? Some examples:

- Are you generous?

- Do you love? Can you give love?

- Do you feel compassion?

- Are you good at something?

- Are you a good listener?

- Do you empathize with the pain of others?

- Do you appreciate beauty in nature, in others?

- Do you have good ideas?

- Are you determined?

- Are you good at sports?

- Are you creative?

And so on. These (and more) are all internal qualities you might have that you can appreciate, that can make you happy about yourself.

So the happiness process—noticing, appreciating, being happy about living—can be applied to things within us, no matter what's going on outside. We can learn to notice and appreciate the good things (and the less-than-perfect things as well!) in ourselves, and start to love ourselves.

Appreciating All That's Around Us

That's just the start, though. What's within us is amazing, but so is what's in everyone else, and life all around us. These might be external things, but the appreciation for them (and the happiness that results) comes from within.

So the key skill is to learn to notice, accept and appreciate everything around us, and everyone we see and interact with.

Look closely at the food you eat, and the coffee, water, tea, or wine you drink . . . what do you notice? Is there good to be noticed that you can appreciate, that can make you happy to be alive?

What about the room around you? What about the book you're reading, or the blog post? What about the nature outside? Are there things there that you can notice and appreciate?

Often if we fail to see good in things or people around us (or ourselves), it's a failure to pay close attention. If the person near you seems rude or uninteresting, you're not paying close enough attention to the details: Are they also funny, or talented, or shy but with hidden secrets? Are they in pain and in need of compassion? Look closer, and see what you can find.

Once you begin to pay attention, and to look, you'll find some amazing things. All around us are examples of beauty, creativity, inspiration, triumph, pain, joy, life.

And once you get good at this, you can start to appreciate the "not-so-perfect" things as well. We judge other people's flaws, and our own flaws, as "bad" . . . but what if they're just a part of being human? Then aren't the "flaws" a celebration of who we are as humans? Aren't anger and rudeness and mistakes a part of our beauty as human beings?

I've been learning to appreciate the "flaws" in my children, for example, as beautiful, as part of the signature of who they are. My little daughter is loud and bold, while my youngest son is quiet(er) but full of motion and adventure. They are different, and those differences are part of what makes each of them wonderful in their own way. If we didn't have these "flaws," we wouldn't be as wonderful.

And this is true, of course, of ourselves. We all have flaws, and we should celebrate them. Notice them, yes, but appreciate them, and use them as reasons to be happy to be alive.

Once we can do this, we can see the wonder in every little thing around us, and inside us. And then we realize that life is a true joy, in every moment, if we simply pay attention and appreciate it.

Action steps: Take a minute to think about the things that have annoyed you, disappointed you, angered you, frustrated you in the recent past. How can you find the awesomeness in those things?

Our Reactions to
the Actions of Others

Frustrations from others can ruin our day—from getting angry at other drivers when they rudely cut you off, to being frustrated with your child or spouse, to being irritated with co-workers, to being offended by a stranger or waiter or rude flight attendant.

The frustration, anger, irritation and being offended—these don't help us. They lead to us acting in a way that's destructive of our relationships with others, in a way that isn't compassionate, calm, understanding. They lead to us not being trusted by others, making others angry, making others not like us. And just as bad, they lead to us feeling bad, which doesn't make for a good day.

If these feelings aren't useful, what should we do? We can't just flip a switch and turn them off, nor can we suppress them (we can try, but it doesn't work).

Start with awareness—to change our reactions, we must first be aware when these reactions happen. You can't change them if you're in automatic mode.

Once you notice it, the key thing is not to act—it's OK to have the feeling, but the action is what is usually destructive. Acting in anger means you're going to do something not kind, not helpful.

So give yourself some space. Walk away, calm down, breathe. The space is where you can watch the emotion rise, peak, fade away. Then you can think about it calmly and act in an appropriate manner. That's what we really want: an appropriate response.

What's an appropriate response? If you take away the anger, the feeling offended, you can respond in a way that makes sense for the situation. For example:

- If someone cuts you off, slow down and give them some space. Maneuver around them if you like, when it's safe. Don't do anything aggressive, and don't let yourself get too worked up.

- If your kid misbehaves, instead of yelling, you can try to understand why, and talk to them about it in a compassionate way, and model good behavior.

- If a co-worker is irritating, you can talk to him calmly, in a collaborative way, instead of a me-vs.-you way.

We Are All Learning

This is a slogan I use to help me put things in perspective: "We are all learning." You can tell it to yourself whenever someone does something you don't like.

What does it mean? If someone is rude, it just means he has a lot to learn about being considerate or managing his anger. If my co-worker screws up, she has some things to learn about the work. If my child screws up or acts badly, she also has a lot to learn about life.

And that's OK. We all have things to learn. We are all in the process of learning, all the time. We're at different stages with different skills, but none of us has learned everything. And if we realize this, we can then be patient with this fellow learner, who after all, can't be expected to know everything and be perfect, right?

We can use this with ourselves as well—when we mess up or react badly, we can forgive ourselves by saying, "We are all learning." We are just as imperfect as everyone else.

When someone does something less than perfectly, rudely, inconsiderately, inappropriately—just tell yourself, "We are all learning." And then smile.

The Other Person Isn't the Problem

This one is more of a ninja-level skill, so don't worry if you don't incorporate this right away.

Here's the thing to ponder: The other person is never the problem.

What does that mean? If someone behaves rudely and you get angry with him, the problem isn't the other person's actions . . . it's your reaction. Or more accurately, it's not even your reaction, but your action based on that reaction.

This point of view contends that other people's actions are just an outside stimulus, just like a leaf falling outside, or a rock falling in front of us on a mountain path. When a rock falls in front of us, we don't get mad at the rock. We go around it. When a leaf falls, we don't think it's being rude to us. We just watch it, and think of it as a natural phenomena.

Other people's actions are really no different. Consider this story, from the Zen tradition:

A man is rowing a boat and sees another person rowing a boat toward him. The boat bumps into his, and he start yelling at the other man, mad that the man bumped into his boat.

Then consider this alternative version:

The same man is rowing a boat and sees an empty boat coming towards him. The boat bumps into his, but he simply steers his boat around it.

In the first version, he gets mad. In the second, he reacts appropriately.

Here's the thing: the boat is always empty. Even when there's another person causing the stimulus, that person isn't trying to do anything to us. They are doing their own thing, motivated by whatever they're going through, and so we shouldn't take it so personally.

When we take things personally, we get angry. When we see the external event as an empty rowboat, we react appropriately.

And so, the other person isn't the problem. It's us taking things personally. This takes time to learn, in your gut instead of just as an idea, but it makes a ton of difference.

Action step: Write down three phrases to say to yourself whenever you have a bad reaction to the actions of others: "Give your reaction some space. We are all learning. The other person isn't the problem." Have these phrases in a place you can see them the next time you might react to someone, and start saying them (silently) to yourself when you notice your reaction to their actions.

Don't Tie Your Self-Worth to Others' Actions

Getting better at reacting to the actions of others is one thing, but one of the more difficult problems is allowing the actions of others to affect how we judge ourselves.

A good example: your boyfriend dumps you, so you wonder what's wrong with yourself. Why doesn't he love you? You opened yourself up to him, you shared your innermost self, you gave all your love to him . . . and he rejected you. This must mean he found you unworthy, right?

Actually, no: His actions have nothing to do with you, really.

Let me emphasize that because it's really important: the actions of other people have very little to do with you.

If your boyfriend rejects you, or your boss gets mad at you, or your friend is a little distant today, that has very

little to do with you (and your value as a person) and everything to do with what's going on with them. They might
be having a bad day, a bad week, are caught up in some
story going on in their heads, are afraid of commitment or
being rejected themselves, fear failing in the relationship,
and so on and so on.

myself

There are a million possible reasons someone might do
something, and they are not a judgment on you. They are
more a statement of what's going on with the other person.
Let's take a few examples:

- *Your friend isn't as attentive as you'd like him to be.*
  Does that mean he doesn't care about you, or doesn't
  want you to be happy? No. It's possible he's just tired,
  or too caught up in things that happened today to
  be attentive. Maybe he's bothered by something you
  did, but that really is more about his issue of dealing with your actions than it is about you as a person. Maybe you can help him deal with that issue,
  or somehow ease his pain.

- *Your co-worker gets irritated with you and is rude.*
  Does that mean you aren't a good person? No, it
  means that person has a short temper and isn't good
  at dealing with other people, or again, might be having a bad day. Instead of taking it personally, see how
  you can either give that person space to cool down,
  or help the person deal with his issues.

- *Someone doesn't get as excited about your idea as you'd* *hoped.* Does their rejection of your idea or proposal mean that you aren't good? No. It's possible your idea isn't great, but that doesn't mean you aren't good or that you don't have good ideas—maybe this is just not the right idea right now. But it's also likely that it's a good idea but that this person doesn't appreciate it, or their interests don't align with this idea right now, or maybe they have other priorities and can't deal with this idea. Instead, thank them and move on to someone else who might be interested.

Those are just a few examples, but you can see how we often take other people's actions personally even when they have very little to do with us. And we can often interpret their actions to be a judgment on us, and so feel bad about ourselves when really it's nothing to do with us.

So how do we deal with other people's actions instead? Let's take a look.

How to Deal with Others' Actions

So someone rejects you, gets mad at you, is indifferent to you, is rude to you . . . what do you do?

There are many options, of course, but here's what I suggest generally:

1. *Don't take it personally.* Their actions don't have anything to do with you, so if you find yourself taking it as a personal affront to you, or a judgment of your worth, be aware of that, and let it go. Tell yourself that this has nothing to do with you, and everything to do with them.

2. *Reaffirm your value.* If you feel yourself doubting your value because of their actions, recognize that your value isn't determined by their actions or judgments. It's determined by you. So reaffirm that you believe you have great value—appreciate the things about yourself that are good and that have value. Even if no one else appreciates you, be the one person who can see those good things and is grateful for them. That's all you need.

3. *Be compassionate.* If that person is mad, rude, irritated, tired or afraid, they are in pain. They might be lashing out at you, or withdrawing from you, because of that pain. See if you can help relieve the pain. You've already checked in with yourself, and realized you are good to go. Now go help the other person. If they don't want your help, that's OK too. Your worth isn't determined by whether someone wants or uses your help—it's the fact that you tried to help that's a statement of your value. You can't control

whether other people receive your help or are grateful for it, but you can at least make the attempt.

These three steps, by the way, don't just help you with your self worth, they also help your relationship with the other person. Often we react to others as if they personally injured us, and the other person doesn't understand why and so they, in turn, take our reaction personally and get mad or hurt. If instead we don't take their actions personally and seek to help them, they are more likely to be grateful than mad or hurt. And so we're better friends, co-workers, partners and parents if we take things less personally and are more compassionate.

Action step: These skills, like all life skills, take practice. Take a minute to replay in your head a recent incident when you were hurt by someone close to you, even just a little, and think about how you might have internalized it into your self image. Now replay the incident in your head in a new way, imagining yourself using the three steps above. Practice this replaying skill at first, and then try to put it into practice when you feel the process happening in the future.

Become Whole In a Relationship

Let's take an example of a woman who spends a lot of her day wondering what her boyfriend is doing, looking for clues that he loves her, wondering why he isn't paying attention to her, worrying that he's flirting with other girls on some social network.

(Note that this applies to both men and women; I've just chosen a woman in this example.)

She's not happy in this relationship—she's dependent on him for her happiness, and unhappy when he's not providing the validation she needs, when he doesn't show how much he loves her. She's insecure, jealous, needy. This doesn't make for a good relationship, or a happy person.

What happens when you have some degree of this in your relationship? You're not a good boyfriend, girlfriend, spouse. The other person feels like he (or she) has to keep making you happy, always be "on" so that you won't wonder what's wrong with your relationship, always supply your needs, never have the freedom to do his own thing while you do yours. This makes for a tough relationship, and if it lasts more than a few years, long-term problems usually develop.

I know because I've done it myself, and had to learn the hard way that this doesn't work well. Almost everyone I know who has had relationship problems has had some of these same issues. And the people who have healthy long-term relationships have found a way to be whole, independent, secure.

So let's take a look at how to become whole in a relationship, and in the process, be happier and be a better partner.

What a Whole Person Looks Like

Before we can talk about relationships, we have to focus on one person, because when you have two people the equation gets a little more complicated. Let's take the simplest part of the equation first—just you.

When you're whole, you don't need someone else's validation to be happy—because you accept yourself. You don't need someone else to love you in order to feel loved—because you love yourself. That's not to say you don't love to be loved by others, or want others in your life, but you already provide the foundation of what you need, all by yourself, by accepting and loving yourself.

When you're whole, you are not insecure, because you aren't worried so much about the other person leaving. Sure, it would be a great loss for your loved one to abandon you, but you'd be fine on your own. You wouldn't be "alone" because you have the best company in the world—yourself. You know you'd survive, be happy, do great things, even without that person. That's not to say you don't want your lover to stay—but you aren't always afraid of the possibility of that person leaving.

When you're whole, you don't need the other person to check in with you all the time because you're happy on your own. You're OK if they go do their own thing, because you're secure in your relationship and you're perfectly fine doing your own thing too. You don't need reassurance of that person's love because you're secure.

Two Whole People Coming Together

A solid relationship is two whole (or at least, fairly whole) people coming together because they love each other's company. They're not coming together because they need someone to love them all the time, because they need someone's company all the time, because they need to be shown that they're loved.

If one person is whole but the other person is needy, dependent, insecure . . . the whole person will do the best that he or she can to help the other, but over the long run will feel weary of all the neediness and insecurity, and will feel resentment. If both are needy and insecure, there will be constant fights about why you didn't check in with me, why you're so distant today, why you're talking to that guy, what you're doing when you go out with your friends, etc.

But if both people are whole, they can be apart and are secure enough not to worry about the other person, and are happy being alone. They can come together and be happy, enjoying each other's company. They don't need each other, but they love each other and care for the other person's happiness—not worrying so much about their own happiness, because they are secure that they're already happy.

The respect each other, and themselves. They are compassionate for each other, and themselves.

This is a relationship with two whole people.

Becoming Whole

So what if you're not this "whole" person, and want to be? Realize you already have everything you need to be whole—you just need to let go of the insecurities, and realize how amazing you already are. You don't need improvement—you need to realize that the awesomeness is already there.

How do you let go of the insecurities? That's not so easy, because it's a slow healing process, but it starts by recognizing them when they appear, and then letting them go. Notice that you're worried about what your significant other is doing, and then recognize that you're worried they don't love you as much as they should, and that means you are worried you're not good enough . . . then let go of that worry. You don't need it. You are good enough.

If you're good enough, that means the other person will either recognize that and love you, or won't recognize it (and therefore won't be deserving of you) and will not love you, but you'll be fine because you're OK on your own. If you're good enough, you'll be good enough with or without this person. That's not to say you want the person to leave, or don't care about the person, but you know that you'd be OK if they did leave you.

Knowing that, you're OK no matter what: whether that person is on a trip, out with friends, working late, even angry with you. You're good, as you are, on your own, and you don't need anything else.

When worries about whether you're good enough crop up, recognize them, let them go. When worries about whether the other person loves you crop up, recognize them, let them go. When fears of the other person flirting with someone else crop up, recognize them, let them go (worst-case scenario: the person cheats, you leave them, you're OK on your own).

Recognize the fears and worries, and let them go. Relax into this new space of being OK with yourself, being happy on your own, knowing things will always be OK.

Once you've learned this wholeness, you can come together with someone else with confidence, love, compassion, security.

Action step: Take a minute to consider your current or recent relationships—possibly with a romantic partner/spouse, but also possibly with a good friend or family member. Have there been times of dependence, insecurity, jealousy, a lack of trust, neediness? Or is it characterized by independence and security? If insecurity and neediness are a problem, what fears are holding you back? Can you let them go?

Self-Happiness and Meeting Others

If becoming whole and happy with yourself helps in a romantic relationship with someone else, what about when it comes to meeting new friends, or making an impression at work or with clients?

It works exactly the same way.

Being happy with yourself means that when you meet other people, you don't need them. You're not desperate for them to like you. You can be happy with them, or without them. However, a person who is happy with himself can also come together with other people and have fun, enjoy a good conversation, make a connection.

Not needing someone's approval doesn't mean you don't want to connect with them. However, it makes it more likely that if you do connect with them, you'll make a good impression. People tend to back off if you're too needy, if you really want their approval . . . but they respect some-one who has approved themselves (not that you have to be cocky—just happy with who you are).

When we don't think we are very likable people, we worry about the impression we're going to leave on other people. This worry comes across to the other person, and makes that person think you don't like yourself, that you might have something to hide, that you're not trustworthy, not open and genuine.

But if you think that you're likable and have something to offer, you can be open, authentic and smile. You aren't afraid to show yourself as you are because you already know you're good. And this comes across to others, and they tend to like this.

So being whole and happy with yourself makes it easier to meet new friends, to get hired for a new job, to make a good impression on your co-workers, to work with clients. In short, it makes any relationship better.

How to Bring Your Happiness to the Table

So what if you're not confident yet in yourself and your abilities? How do you go out and meet people and know that you have something to bring to the conversation and relationship?

Here's the key: Start with the base realization that you don't need any person's approval, and that you are fine even without it. This is true: If someone else doesn't like you, your life isn't ruined. You can be happy going for a walk, reading a book, writing a novel, doing a workout, laying in the grass, watching the sunset. You can be happy just with yourself.

Once you start with that realization, you can let go of the worries about what other people will think of you. When the insecurities come up (they will out of habit), realize that they stem from wanting the approval of another person, and then remember that you don't need that approval. You're fine without it. The desire for approval is causing you pain, and you don't need that pain.

This process can happen repeatedly, but you get better at letting it go. Also focus on the things about yourself that you like, the talents you have, the things you have to offer. Appreciate these things about yourself. Know that you're worthy of anyone's attention and trust.

This confidence will come with practice because when you meet someone and they like you because you aren't trying to get their approval, you will begin to trust the process.

Does this mean you should brag about yourself when you meet with people? Not at all—someone who needs approval will give you their accomplishments and show their good side. Someone who doesn't need approval will be happy to listen to another person, will try to get to know the other person and will also be willing to share all the sides of who they are, not just the good side.

The amazing thing is that this openness and willingness to share vulnerabilities is a powerful way to build trust. When you can open up and share the parts of you that aren't absolutely flattering because you aren't worried about being judged, the other person will trust you much more and will also feel like opening up. This creates a much more genuine connection.

Action step: Make a list of the things you like about yourself, your talents, your strengths. Take a moment with each item and appreciate that one thing about yourself. Keep this list for regular reminder sessions so you slowly grow to know your worth and are happy with who you are.

Jealousy of Others

Have you ever seen something exciting that a friend is doing on some social network and felt a pang of jealousy? Or heard travel stories from people you know—amazing stories of exotic places—and wished it had been you living those adventures, going to those parties?

Jealousy of others is a widespread phenomenon, and social media seems to increase the tendency in us. It can manifest in so many ways: jealousy of someone's nice stomach or sculpted arms, a feeling that you're missing out on all the fun other people are having, a worry that other people are doing cooler things than you in business, a wish that you could have the love life or sex life of someone you know.

Contentment is obviously the antidote.

If you are content with who you are, you don't need someone else's nice stomach or love life or business accomplishments. If you are content with what you're doing, you don't need to worry about all the fun everyone else is having, the beautiful food photos they're taking of lunch, the travel photos that show the highlights of their lives (compared to the everyday moments of your life).

Action step: Stop comparing your life with anyone else's life. Stop comparing who you are or how you look with anyone else. This is easier said than done: It takes a process of awareness, and when you notice the comparison, pause. Instead of looking outward, at what other people are doing, look at what you're doing and appreciate it. When you notice something good about someone else that makes you jealous, stop, and look at yourself instead—what can you appreciate?

Techniques for Self-Acceptance

Contentment is largely determined by our level of self-acceptance. But how do you actually learn self-acceptance?

Let's look at some techniques that will help you learn how to accept all of yourself—the "good" and the "bad." These are variations on a theme, but try one for a few days, then try another, and with time you'll develop a strong self-acceptance skillset.

The Techniques

1. *Practice relaxed awareness.* What is relaxed awareness? As opposed to constant distraction, or concentrated focus, relaxed awareness is a soft consciousness of our thoughts, feelings, pain, self-rating and judgment, etc. It's an awareness of our existence, and the stream of phenomena that is occurring at this moment, including thoughts and emotions and outside stimuli.

To practice, close your eyes for a minute, and instead of pushing thoughts away or trying to focus on your breath, just softly notice your thoughts and feelings and body. You might see negative thoughts or emotions—that's OK. Just notice them, watch them. Don't try to turn them into positive thoughts or push them away. You can do this practice for 5 minutes a day, or up to 30 minutes if you find it useful.

2. *Welcome what you notice.* When you practice relaxed awareness, you'll notice things—negative thoughts, fears, happy thoughts, self-judgments, etc. We tend to want to stop the negative thoughts and feelings, but this is just a suppression, an avoidance, a negating of the negative. Instead, welcome these phenomena, invite them in for a cup of tea, give them a hug. They are a part of your life, and they are OK. If you feel bad about how you've been doing with exercise, that's OK. Hug the bad feeling, comfort it, let it hang around for awhile. They are not bad, but are opportunities to learn things about ourselves. When we run from these "bad" feelings, we create more pain. Instead, see the good in them, and find the opportunity. Be OK with them.

3. *Let go of rating yourself.* Another thing you'll notice, once you start to pay attention, is self-rating. We

rate ourselves compared to others, or rate ourselves as "good" or "bad" at different things, or rate ourselves as flabby or too skinny or ugly. This is not a very useful activity. That doesn't mean to let it go, but just to notice it, and see what results from it. After realizing that self-rating repeatedly causes you pain, you'll be happy to let it go, in time. Gratitude sessions. Wake up in the morning and think about what you're grateful for. Include things about yourself. If you failed at something, what about that failure are you grateful for? If you aren't perfect, what about your imperfection can you be grateful for? Feel free to journal about these things each day, or once a week if that helps.

4. *Compassion and forgiveness for yourself.* As you notice judgments and self-rating, see if you can turn them into forgiveness and compassion. If you judge yourself for not doing well at something, or not being good enough at something, can you forgive yourself for this, just as you might forgive someone else? Can you learn to understand why you did it, and see that ultimately you don't even need forgiveness? If we really seek to understand, we realize that we did the best we could, given our human-ness, environment, what we've learned and practiced, etc. And so we don't need to forgive, but instead to understand, and seek to do things that might relieve the pain.

5. *Learn from all parts.* We tend to try to see our successes as good, and the failures as bad, but what if we see that everything is something to learn from? Even the dark parts—they are parts of us, and we can find interesting and useful things in them too.

6. *Separate from your emotions.* When you are feeling negative emotions, see them as a separate event, not a part of you, and watch them. Remove their power over you by thinking of them not as commandments you must follow or believe in, but rather passing objects, like a leaf floating past you in the wind. The leaf doesn't control you, and neither do negative emotions.

7. *Talk to someone.* This is one of my favorite techniques. We get so in our heads that it's difficult to separate our thoughts and emotions, to see things clearly. Talking through these issues with another person—a friend, spouse, co-worker—can help you to understand yourself better. Use the talking technique together with one of the above techniques.

As you learn self-acceptance, realize that it is always available to you, and you can have it no matter what you do. You can learn, create interesting things and make connections with others, with self-acceptance at the center of that. It can change everything you do, if you practice.

Action step: Set a reminder once a day to practice one of the techniques above. Do it for a week, then switch to another step. With daily practice, these skills become second nature.

Frequently Asked Questions

To finish off this book, I'd like to answer some questions submitted by you, my wonderful readers. They are excellent questions!

The first section seems to be the greatest concern for most people on the topic of contentment—contentment vs. self-improvement, or contentment vs. complacency. I understand this concern, as it was one of the things I debated in my own head as I started to explore contentment. I'll address those related questions first, and then get to the others below.

Contentment vs. Complacency or Self-Improvement

How does being content in life fit in with the human need to grow and help?

Leo: The need to grow and help doesn't go away if you learn to be content with yourself and your life. For example,

I am content with who I am, but I also love learning new things. It's not necessary to be discontented with yourself or life in order to love learning new things. Same goes with helping other people. In fact, in my experience, you are more likely to help other people and have fun learning new things if you are content with who you are.

I've been wondering about how you balance the art of contentment with wanting to improve yourself and your life. It seems to me that some people (most people?) almost need a certain amount of dissatisfaction in order to be able to make changes . . . but I'm sure there is a balance to be found there. Would love to hear your take.

Leo: Actually, the dissatisfaction turns out to be unnecessary. I think we all believe that change can only come from a place of being unhappy with how things are, but it turns out that's not true at all. Contentment and change are not mutually exclusive. An example:

I've been a student of Zen for over 25 years so I definitely understand the value of contentment and living now vs. always striving and churning, but I also understand that there is no such thing as standing still. How do you keep contentment from turning to complacency and back sliding? I know that I do it by oscillating from achievement and improvement to periods of enjoying life as it is. The problem is that I tend to get stuck in one mode or the other for extended periods of time. Any advice?

Leo: There's definitely a fine-tuning of finding balance, but I suggest combining the two modes—achievement/improvement and enjoying life as it is. They are completely compatible with each other. Enjoy life as it is, which includes the desire to help people (which can drive achievement) and the love of learning (which can drive improvement). You don't have to put off enjoying life right now in order to love helping people or love learning (or love other things that might drive achievement or improvement). It's true that achievement/improvement can be driven by dissatisfaction, but it's not mandatory.

Many people would say contentment is a nicer word for mediocrity. Is it?

Leo: No, that comes from a misunderstanding of what contentment is. It's not being lazy and doing nothing. It's being happy and enjoying what you're doing, which can include doing good work.

How do you uncouple contentment from complacency? Contentment is wonderful - complacency is dangerous.

Leo: Having a commitment to people helps a lot. For example, I have a commitment to my readers to helping and being trustworthy and delivering articles of a certain standard (in my mind at least). I can be content but still want to fulfill that commitment, and also to maintain our relationship with each other. Those are good things, and you can do them even if you're content.

Balance is a big one. Present contentment vs. future goals. What makes your loved ones happy vs. what makes you happy.

Leo: Contentment can be present during all the other stuff—it doesn't exclude goals or making others happy. For example, I can be content with myself and my life but still want to help others, and so my future goal can be to build new schools in Southeast Asia. My goal is driven by a love of helping, rather than a lack of contentment. Making others happy can happen at the same time as being happy myself, so they aren't exclusive. But yes, finding a balance between different activities is always something we'll work with, even if we find contentment.

In my humble opinion, contentment is contrary to the human condition. We have an innate desire for more. Maslow described this in his hierarchy of needs model. We are never truly content until we reach self actualization. Take the example of the rich 1% movie stars. Although they have no struggle for material things most are never content. In fact, many are miserable and resort to drugs and other addictions in an attempt to satisfy. I guess your book will address how to be content with what we have already.

Leo: It's definitely contrary to our cultural condition. But many people around the world, in poor conditions and in what we would call "tribal" conditions, have been found to be content, so it's hard to argue that it's contrary to the human condition. Sure, it's hard to be content if you don't have the first few levels of Maslow's hierarchy fulfilled. But the truth is there is no prerequisite for contentment—you always have the raw materials for it, which is your mind. You only need to appreciate what's inside you, and all around you, and that can be done no matter where you are or what your life circumstances are.

Other Great Questions

How do you neutralize FOMO? (fear of missing out)?

Leo: Great question! Fear of Missing Out (FOMO) is at the heart of what contentment is. When we fear missing out, what are we really worried about? We are afraid that we're not going to be a part of something important/exciting/fun/etc. This stems from an ideal in our heads: that we can be a part of everything important, exciting and fun. Of course, this is not ever true; it's only a fantasy. When we realize this, we can instead turn our attention to what's in front of us—what we have, who we are, what we're doing, who we're with. These things are amazing, and we only need to appreciate them to be content. This is the same process that we use to fight other fears and dissatisfaction.

What about contentment when your significant other / spouse / partner / family member is generally not content? How to deal with others' discontent, or how to not let their discontent influence your aim to be content?

Leo: It is difficult, but definitely a skill worth learning. Honestly, I'm still learning myself, but what little I've learned has helped tremendously. See the chapters titled, "Our Reactions to the Actions of Others" and "Don't Tie Your Self-Worth to Others' Actions," and learn to focus on your reaction to your spouse or family member's words or actions toward you. You can work with your reaction, no matter what their actions are. Another way to shift your focus in this situation is to focus on compassion for the other person—they are discontented, which means they are suffering. You definitely know what that's like, and it's not fun. So be compassionate, empathize with their suffering, and see if there's a way you can help (without being patronizing, of course).

How do you respond to people who push you to do more, get more, be more when you are content with who and where you are?

Leo: Smile, and give them a hug. What we have to learn is that no matter how content we've learned to be, there will always be people who expect us to act differently, who push us or get angry with us or make us feel guilty. That's OK. That's the way of the world, and we can never change that. The only thing we can change is how we handle it. So I suggest learning to empathize with these people, smile, and give them a hug. It might not change how they try to push us, but it might, and more importantly, we have changed our reaction to them.

Sometimes I think we live in a world of too many choices. I also think the average person's relentless pursuit of all things material can foster this idea of people never knowing the idea/concept of contentment.

Leo: Two great concepts in one question! First, too many choices is a definite challenge—it helps to have some principles to guide you, like the principle of compassion and helping others, the principle of curiosity, the principle of building relationships. But even then, you'll be uncertain about choices, and the idea is to be OK with the uncertainty (it's a great part of life), and just choose, and let go of the worry you made the right choice (it doesn't help). There's never going to be a certainty that you made the right choice. You can only try it, see what happens, and learn. So put away the menu after you've ordered, forget about it, and you'll be happier.

Second, the relentless pursuit of material things . . . yes, it can get in the way of understanding or even contemplating contentment. Corporations intentionally make us dissatisfied with our lives or ourselves in some way, so that we'll buy their solution (a car, new shoes, a new gadget). And so we're always pursuing some dream of material happiness, when obviously that doesn't work, and it never ends.

It's a fantasy. We think we need all of that to be happy, but it doesn't make us happy. Instead, we can be happy right now, with what we already have.

I simply find it a challenge to remember to be content with what I've got. Once I remember it is easier.

Leo: Definitely. So how do we remember to be content? It's a mental habit, which can be difficult to form or change. The main way we change a mental habit like this is simply repeated practice. You try today, then forget, then review what happened and realize you forgot, then try again. The repeated trying comes from a commitment—to yourself, but also to others. For example, I told my kids that I am trying to be more mindful as a parent, and compassionate when I talk to them—things I can often forget. They now know that I'm doing this, and are watching me, and that helps me to remember. Also, have reminders. Set a reminder for a gratitude session, which can include a review of what you did that day related to contentment.

How do you deal with other people's expectations? I'm a stay at home mum and very happy to be able to spend that time with my two year old son. People constantly ask me when I am going to start working. It seems like the "normal" thing to do. Truly, I'm content to keep things as they are, but expectations from other people leave me feeling guilty.

Leo: It's incredibly important that we learn to deal internally with other people's expectations, because those will always be there, no matter what we do. We could try to conform with their expectations, but even then, there would be other expectations we aren't meeting, and who wants to conform with everyone else's expectations? So we need to let go of the ideal of everyone approving of what we're doing, because it's unachievable. Instead, work internally with this, let go of it, and appreciate the greatness of what you're doing and who you are. You then have the approval you want—your own, not other people's.

Lastly, this is also an opportunity to educate people—when they express concern for you, thank them, and then have a conversation about what you're doing and why. It's incredible that they are worried about you—they care! And so you should be grateful for that, but also engage them so that they are moved toward an understanding of what you're doing. It's a long process, so in the meantime, be content and smile.

How to be happy with the work-life balance?

Leo: This is a tough question because people often mean different things when they say "work-life balance." As we know, work is a part of life, so segregating them is artificial and unnecessary. Often what people mean, though, is that they're working too much, and want time for other things. And that's totally legitimate, and you can do things like setting limits on work, making commitments to others (meeting a friend for a walk or run or hike, etc.), carving out time for meditation or yoga, signing up for music or language lessons, etc. But it's also important to be content when you're working, which you can absolutely do following the principles of this book.

I find it a challenge to have contentment with the knowledge I obtained and am frequently seeking more (books, movies, talks, researches) about the most varied subjects. How to have contentment with the knowledge you already have?

Leo: There are two kinds of knowledge seeking: the first is thinking you don't know enough or don't know the important things and so you need to go out and learn (fear of not reaching an ideal knowledge level, which is a fantasy), and the second is being content with what you know, but still being curious about other things, and appreciating your love for learning new things. I suggest the second. Letting go of the fantasy of an ideal knowledge level involves the same process as letting go of other fantasies, explained in this book.

Fundamentally, the difficulties with being content seem to be related to unfulfilled expectations and judgments. Simply put, things are different from what we want them to be. I understand that mindfulness meditation is the most powerful tool to learn to let go, fully appreciate present moment and be content and grateful. Having said that, it seems that it takes a relatively long time to be established in mindfulness firmly enough, so it will generate contentment. It would be really helpful if you could recommend additional practices that are compatible with mindfulness, to work on cultivating contentment more directly.

Leo: Mindfulness is important because it's a prerequisite to working with the ideals and expectations and judgments and comparisons that we always have in our heads, all day long. Unfortunately, we're almost never aware of this process, and so we need to learn to be aware, which is what mindfulness is. We need to turn our attention inward to work with this process. You can do this with meditation or yoga, or you can simply create reminders to pay attention to your thought processes, and turn inward at various times in the day, until you learn to be more mindful of these processes without the reminders.

My problem is GUILT, when I feel content with myself these are experiences usually related to very private moments of self discovery, very hard to explain and share with my loves ones, for whom I look detached. I've found ways to deal with this with my kids and husband, gradually gaining private moments from where I return in peace. But for other relatives and friends I'm consistently ungrateful and distant. To fulfill that need of contentment, in my case, I need a lot of private time, and is fantastic, I've taking most of my 40 years blind to my own needs. But, hurts that my father, sister, cousins and friends see me as an alien. Guilt prevents me from exploring deeper in paths I know are for me.

Leo: Great question. While private time is amazing, perhaps you can shift how you are when you're with other people, so you don't seem distant and ungrateful. Contentment doesn't preclude warmth and compassion and gratitude—in fact, I think they go well together. So work privately on contentment, but when you're with others, engage with them, pay attention, and show gratitude.

How do you find contentment while grieving? And I don't mean the initial grief that comes with the shock of a loss, I mean the slow burn of grief that follows in the months and years after. I feel complacent and resigned now, but any sense of joy or contentment feels fleeting.

Leo: Really important and challenging stuff. I'm not going to pretend it's easy. However, it's useful to look at the inner process that's happening here: Grief is the suffering that comes not from the external loss of someone or something, but from the internal loss of wanting your life to be a certain way (to have a certain someone in your life, for example). I'm not saying this to trivialize your loss or grief, but to show what we all do when we grieve. We are mourning the loss of an ideal, the loss of what we believed ourselves to be. If we can recognize this, we can let go of that ideal, because the truth is, there is no one thing our lives will be, no one self we'll ever be. It's always changing.

Embrace that change, and see the good in it. It might seem horrible to imply that we should be happy that someone is gone (I'm not saying that), but it's important to be able to embrace the changes in life (and changes of self). So one person is not in our lives anymore, which is sad, but that's an opportunity to reinvent our lives and ourselves, to find out what we're like in this new changed reality. Again, this is difficult stuff, but really powerful to learn, because in truth it happens all the time, on different levels.

How to remain content despite past bad decisions which consequences you have to live with for the rest of your life? Some kind of bad decisions you can't leave behind because you have to face them every day and affect your day-by-day.

Leo: There will always be bad decisions, and their consequences—we can't ever get rid of them or change them. The only thing we can change is our mindset toward them, our reactions to them. So one way to look at bad decisions is that it's all part of the learning process, which is a good thing. We want to learn, and making mistakes is part of how we really learn something. Embrace mistakes as part of this great process. Another way to look at the consequences of your past decisions: They are just external stimulus, and they are only bad because we are comparing them to an ideal (we should have done better, which of course is a fantasy because we didn't). If we realize this, we can let go of the ideal (it's hurting us), and instead, focus on appreciating what's right in front of us.

I've always questioned on exactly how to achieve that level of greatness [Note from Leo: I believe this question is referencing my post about Warren Buffett, who is considered one of the greatest investors in history.]. Is it by surrounding yourself around other successful people? By being friendly? How would I be able to find contentment in an area where peace is hard to come across due to the ego differences between other people. Here in New York City, in Queens, people seem paranoid; and closed off to other people. Then the people who talk to other people are labeled as "crazy" or some other label; then at times people remain closed off because it seems like people don't want life experience.

Leo: Surrounding yourself with positive people who will support you, inspire you, hold you accountable for the changes you're making . . . this definitely helps. Building relationships and trust, being trustworthy, genuinely wanting to help other people, getting good at what you do . . . those also help.

Regarding being in an environment where people are closed off to each other, and where you'd stick out for being friendly, this can be difficult. You can change your environment (for example, I moved my family from Guam to San Francisco, for many reasons), or you can build up a support network online, where you're not limited by the people who are physically around you. I believe that if you're friendly and compassionate and helpful, you'll also find other people like that in your neighborhood, even if most people judge you (that's OK).

I'm wondering about how to find contentment in this busy time as a student before final exams. To be content with hard decisions of choosing to leave the loved ones and go study abroad or to stay and study local . . .

Leo: You can be busy and content. Contentment is just a happiness with yourself and your life, and so you can feel this as you study and take exams, even if you're busy. Making hard decisions will always be hard, even if you're content. The trick is to be content with the decision after you make it, and let go of worry that you made the wrong choice, while paying attention and seeing how the choice is working out, learning about yourself in the process.

How to let it be okay . . . when things are "okay". (Have issues with allowing life to be smooth . . . rocky has been the norm for so very long it's become my bff.)

Leo: We fall into mental habits, like wanting excitement or emotional "drama," or equating happiness and excitement, and when you do something like that for so long it becomes normal. It's good that you recognize this, because many people don't. However, we can let go of those mental habits, with awareness and practice. When things are

OK, focus on appreciating the beauty of that peace, rather than wanting the excitement or drama that you've come to be used to. When you notice yourself expecting rockiness, watch this, and then focus again on appreciating what you have. It takes repeated practice.

Conclusion

Contentment is a super power. If you can learn the skills of contentment, your life will be better in so many ways:

- You'll enjoy life more.

- Your relationships will be stronger.

- You'll be better at meeting people.

- You'll be healthier, and good at forming healthy habits.

- You'll like and trust yourself more.

- You'll be jealous less.

- You'll be less angry and more at peace.

- You'll be happier with your body.

- You'll be happier no matter what you're doing or who you're with.

Those are a lot of benefits, from one small bundle of skills. Putting some time in learning the skills of contentment is worth the effort and will pay off for the rest of your life.

But if learning contentment seems out of reach, overwhelming . . . realize that you can be happy right now, as you're learning. Each step of the way, not just at the end.

How can you be happy right now, and each step along the way? By enjoying the process. By not looking so far down the road, but appreciating the joys of what you're doing right now, and the good things about yourself in this moment. That's something you can do right this moment, and it's available at any moment.

The Skills of Contentment

So what are the skills of contentment? We've gone over them throughout this book, but to summarize, they are:

1. *Awareness*. Notice when you're making comparisons, when you have ideals and fantasies and expectations, when they are making you less content and causing pain.

2. *Acceptance*. Don't beat yourself up about it, and accept that this process is happening. It's part of life.

Accept it, and face it, and find the appropriate, non-emotional response.

3. *Letting go of comparisons.* When you notice the comparisons, accept that you've made them, but realize that they are hurting you, and that they are completely unnecessary. You can let go of them, and be perfectly fine.

4. *Compassion.* Compassion for yourself—this is how you let go of the ideals and comparisons. They are hurting you, making you less happy, and so it's a compassionate act to let go of them. Let them be.

5. *Appreciation.* Instead of comparing and holding onto ideals, focus instead on appreciating what you have, who you're with, what you're doing, and who you are. Find the good in each thing, including in yourself.

6. *Loving yourself, and everything else too.* Once you've found the good to appreciate, in yourself or anything/anybody around you, learn to love it. This is the beauty of life, and it is incredible.

These are the key skills, and they'll help you with pretty much any of the problems we talked about in this book—unhealthy habits, jealousy, feeling bad about yourself, bad relationships, debt and procrastination and much more.

They take time to learn. One small step at a time, you can learn them. And enjoy yourself each small step along the way.

It is my immense privilege to be talking to you about these skills, these challenges you face, this central principle of a good life. I have confidence that you can learn these skills, and that they'll profoundly change your life. Thank you, for reading this book to the end, and for your attention.

It is appreciated.

Summary of Action Steps

I've compiled a list of all the action steps at the end of each chapter, to make it easier for you to practice them on a regular basis:

1. Think about the problems you might have, and try to see how discontent is at the root of each problem.

2. Ask yourself if you're content right now. If not, when do you want to be content? What's stopping you?

3. Consider what ideals you have that you compare yourself to. Also ask yourself if you trust yourself to be able to follow through, to stick to changes, to get things done.

4. Think about the things about yourself that you want to change. Then see if, instead, you can find things about yourself you're really happy with.

5. Think about the times you've compared yourself to others, and what others are doing, especially recently. Where did you get the image of others that you're comparing yourself to? Social media or apps, news, blogs, movies, magazines?

6. Make a note to watch when you're frustrated, disappointed, angry, stressed, unhappy . . . and to write down, at that moment, what fantasy you're having. Practice letting them go.

7. Examine one of your made-up needs, and ask yourself why it's such an important need. Ask what would happen if you dropped it. What good would it do? Would you have more free time and more space to concentrate and create, or less stress and fewer things to check off each day? What bad things would happen—or might happen? And how likely is it that these things would happen? And how could you counteract them?

8. Forgive yourself for past mistakes. Before you can start to trust yourself again, you have to go over all your past failures and the bad feelings you have of them. Just take a few minutes right now to do that. Yes, you failed. Yes, that's OK. We all fail. That's no reason to feel bad about yourself. Let it go! Tell yourself that you are good, that mistakes were not your fault but rather the fault of the method.

9. Start to make and keep promises with yourself. This part takes longer because trust isn't regained overnight. Make small promises to yourself. Seriously, as small as you can. For example, if your habit is yoga, tell yourself all you need to do is get on the mat. You don't even need to do 5 minutes. Then do everything you can to keep that promise. Same thing for non-habit stuff—just start writing, just get one veggie in your meal, just close your computer for a minute when a timer goes off (if you want to focus on other things besides the Internet, for example). Small promises but big efforts to keep them. Over time, you'll start to learn that you are trustworthy.

10. Take a look in the mirror. What do you see? Do you notice your judgments? Do you notice what you're judging yourself on—what you're comparing yourself to? You might not realize exactly what that fantasy ideal is—but it's based on images in the media and others you've seen in your life. Try looking at your body (and face) without judgment. Accept it for what it is, without thinking, "I wish it were different." It's not different. It's exactly how it is, and that's the perfect version of what it should be. There is no better version.

11. Take a minute to consider your external sources of happiness. What gives you pleasure, makes you

happy, and what happens when these things (or people) aren't available to give you that pleasure? How do you feel? Notice yourself as you seek these forms of pleasure. Notice when you are looking to your significant other for validation or happiness. Notice what happens when you don't have them and how your happiness might go up or down depending on what's going on externally.

12. Remember this truth: Noticing and appreciating the goodness in anything causes us to be happy about living. And the more we notice and appreciate about our lives (and ourselves), the happier we are.

13. The happiness process—noticing, appreciating, being happy about living—can be applied to things outside of us, and also within us, no matter what's going on outside. We can learn to notice and appreciate the good things (and the less-than-perfect things as well!) in ourselves, and start to love ourselves. Take a minute to think about the things that have annoyed you, disappointed you, angered you, frustrated you in the recent past. How can you find the awesomeness in those things?

14. Write down three phrases to say to yourself whenever you have a bad reaction to the actions of others: "Give your reaction some space. We are all learning. The other person isn't the problem." Have these

phrases in a place you can see them the next time you might react to someone, and start saying them (silently) to yourself when you notice your reaction to their actions. See the chapter "Our Reactions to the Actions of Others" for more on these phrases.

15. Don't tie your self-worth to others' actions, because their actions have very little to do with you. Take a minute to replay in your head a recent incident when you were hurt by someone close to you, even just a little, and think about how you might have internalized it into your self image. Now replay the incident in your head in a new way, imagining yourself using the three steps above. Practice this replaying skill at first, and then try to put it into practice when you feel the process happening in the future.

16. Become whole as a person, self-sufficient, and you'll come together with another person in a stronger way. Take a minute to consider your current or recent relationships—possibly with a romantic partner/spouse, but also possibly with a good friend or family member. Have there been times of dependence, insecurity, jealousy, a lack of trust, neediness? Or is it characterized by independence and security? If insecurity and neediness are a problem, what fears are holding you back? Can you let them go?

17. Being happy with yourself will make you more secure when you meet other people. Make a list of the things you like about yourself, your talents, your strengths. Take a moment with each item and appreciate that one thing about yourself. Keep this list for regular reminder sessions so you slowly grow to know your worth and are happy with who you are.

18. Stop comparing your life with anyone else's life. Stop comparing who you are or how you look with anyone else. This is easier said than done: It takes a process of awareness, and when you notice the comparison, pause. Instead of looking outward, at what other people are doing, look at what you're doing and appreciate it. When you notice something good about someone else that makes you jealous, stop, and look at yourself instead—what can you appreciate?

19. Practice the techniques of self-acceptance. Set a reminder once a day to practice one of the techniques in the "Techniques for Self-Acceptance" chapter. Do it for a week, then switch to another step. With daily practice, these skills become second nature.

For More

More resources on finding contentment can be found on Zen Habits at the *Little Book of Contentment page*.

You can read more from me at *Zen Habits*.

You also don't need more.

CPSIA information can be obtained
at www.ICGtesting.com
Printed in the USA
BVOW04s1641221216
471492BV00001B/14/P